ISBN: 9781314473896

Published by:
HardPress Publishing
8345 NW 66TH ST #2561
MIAMI FL 33166-2626

Email: info@hardpress.net
Web: http://www.hardpress.net

THE LIBRARY
OF
THE UNIVERSITY
OF CALIFORNIA

PRESENTED BY
PROF. CHARLES A. KOFOID AND
MRS. PRUDENCE W. KOFOID

Ethel.

Dec. 20th 1894

Frontispiece.]

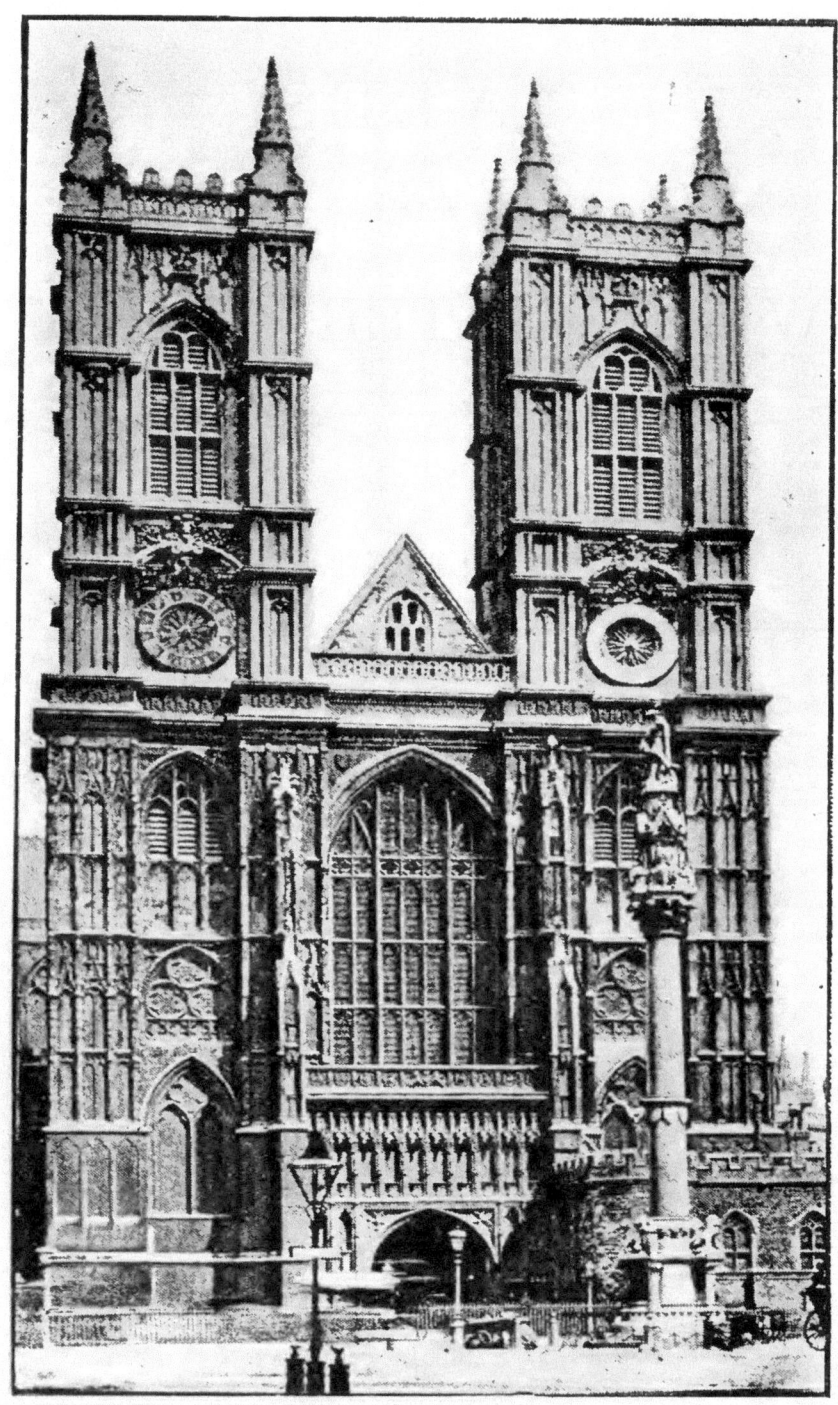

WEST FRONT OF WESTMINSTER ABBEY.
After a Photograph by the London Stereoscopic and Photographic Co., Ltd.

TALES

FROM

WESTMINSTER ABBEY

TOLD TO CHILDREN BY

MRS. FREWEN LORD.

WITH
VIGNETTE PORTRAIT OF DEAN STANLEY, PLAN OF THE ABBEY
AND GENERAL VIEW OF WEST FRONT OF ABBEY.

SECOND EDITION.

LONDON:
SAMPSON LOW, MARSTON & COMPANY
LIMITED,
St. Dunstan's House,
FETTER LANE, FLEET STREET, E.C.
1894.

[*All rights reserved.*]

LONDON:
PRINTED BY WILLIAM CLOWES AND SONS, LIMITED,
STAMFORD STREET AND CHARING CROSS.

DEAN STANLEY.
From a Photograph by the London Stereoscopic Company.

DEDICATED

TO THE MEMORY OF

DEAN STANLEY,

WHOSE WALKS AND TALKS WITH CHILDREN

IN WESTMINSTER ABBEY

CAN NEVER BE EFFACED FROM THE

GRATEFUL RECOLLECTION OF ONE WHO AS A CHILD

HAD THE HAPPINESS OF ENJOYING THEM.

TALES

FROM

WESTMINSTER ABBEY.

CHAPTER I.

A GREAT many years ago, when I was quite a small child, I was taken with some other children over Westminster Abbey by Dean Stanley, who was then the Dean of Westminster.

Some of you may have read a book called "Tom Brown's School Days," and if so you will remember Tom's great friend, Arthur, who began his school life a lonely and home-sick little boy, but who as the years went on came to be looked up to and liked almost more than any other boy at Rugby. "George Arthur" this boy is called in the book, but his real name was Arthur Stanley, and when he grew up he became a clergyman, and was for many years Dean of Westminster. He wrote a great many books, and one all about Westminster Abbey; for he knew every corner and part of this great church, and was full of stories about the great people who are buried here, and the kings and queens who were crowned here. There was nothing he liked better than taking people over the Abbey, and any one who had the happiness of going with him, as I did, and of hearing him, would always remember some, at any rate, of the stories he told.

He died in 1881, and as none of you can ever see or hear him, standing in the Abbey surrounded by children, and telling them all that he thought would interest them, I am going to take out of my memory, and out of this book of his,* just as much of what he used to say as I hope will help you to enjoy what you will see there.

* "Memorials of Westminster Abbey."

When one goes to visit any place for the first time, there is always a great deal that one wants to have explained; and what I myself most enjoy is to read or be told beforehand something about what I am going to see, and then I understand it much better—I do not waste so much time in asking questions, and have all the more time to look about.

If we go and stand at the great West Door, as it is called, of Westminster Abbey, and look down Victoria Street, it is difficult to believe that this very same place was, hundreds of years ago, quite wild country. Where there are now houses and streets and churches, there used to be only marshy land and forests. Where there are now endless streams of carriages, carts, and omnibuses, and people hurrying along, there were in the far-off time, when the Abbey Church of Westminster was first begun, only wild oxen or huge red deer with towering antlers which strayed from the neighbouring hills and roamed about in this jungle. It used to be called "the terrible place," so wild and so lonely was it.

Dotted about in the marsh were many little islands, one of which was called Thorney Isle, because there were so many wild thorn trees growing there, and on this spot Westminster Abbey now stands.

For as the forests in this part of London were gradually cut down, this island looked so pretty and quiet with the water flowing all round it, and nothing to be seen from it but sunny green meadows, that King Edward the Confessor chose it as the place to build a great church, which he called the Church of St. Peter. At that time there were not many large churches in England, and the Church of St. Peter was thought to be one of the most splendid that was ever seen. It took fifteen years to build, but at last it was finished, and on Christmas Day, 1065, King Edward the Confessor, wearing his crown, as was the custom in those days on great occasions, came with all his bishops and nobles to the first great service in the Abbey Church which he himself had built. He was then a very old man, and a few days after the great service he was taken ill and died, and was buried in his own church. He is called the Founder of the Abbey, and you will see, when you go round it, the shrine of King Edward and of his queen, who was afterwards buried at his side.

Now, there is only one more thing to be remembered before we begin to look round inside and decide what are the most interesting things to see, and that is that this Abbey we are in to-day is *not* the actual Church of St. Peter which King Edward the Confessor built. Of that church there is now left only a little bit of one pillar, which perhaps a guide will show you, within the altar-rail, in what is called the "Sacrarium." I do not mean that the church was pulled down all at once, and this Abbey built instead, but bit by bit, as years went on, it was added to and altered. New parts were built on by different kings—for Westminster Abbey is a church that has been all built by kings and princes—and as the new parts were added, the old were gradually pulled down.

Of all the kings who helped to build and beautify the Abbey, Henry III. was the one who did most, and he spent on it such enormous sums of money that he is often spoken of as one of the most extravagant kings England ever had. He made up his mind that the Abbey of Westminster was to be the most beautiful church in the world, and he used to invite the best foreign artists and sculptors to come and help to make plans and paintings and carvings for it. He it was who built the shrine where Edward the Confessor is now buried, in the part of the choir behind where the communion table (formerly the high altar) now stands. It was when he was growing to be an old man that he thought the founder of the Abbey ought to be treated with special honour and respect, and so almost the last thing he did in his life was to build this shrine, which stands in what is called Edward the Confessor's Chapel.

The king sent all the way to Rome—and in those days the journey was a very much longer and more difficult one than it is now—for the mosaics and enamels which are still to be seen on the shrine; the workmen who made it came from Rome, where the best workmen were then to be found; and the twisted columns round the shrine were made in imitation of the columns on some of the tombs in the great churches in Rome.*

When it was finished, in 1269, the old king himself, his brother Richard, and his two sons, Edward and Edmund, carried the coffin of Edward the Confessor on their shoulders from the place where it had been buried in 1065 to the new chapel, and there it has rested to this very day.

Years afterwards a great and magnificent

---

* The Basilicas of St. John Lateran, St. Paul, St. Lorenzo, and St. Clement.

chapel was added by Henry VII. at the east end of the Abbey, which was called after him. He was buried there when he died, and so were his grandson, Edward VI., and Queen Elizabeth, and Mary Queen of Scots, and many others whose tombs you must look at by-and-by.

It was in the year 1509 that Henry VII. was buried in Westminster Abbey, just four hundred and forty-four years after the burial of King Edward the Confessor. But in these four hundred and forty-four years the Abbey had been so much altered, the old parts so pulled down and rebuilt, that King Edward, could he have seen it again, would hardly have believed that this great Abbey, as we see it to-day, had grown up from his first Church of St. Peter on Thorney Isle.

And now, as I have said enough about the building of the Abbey, we can go inside and begin to see some of the monuments and tombs of which it is full.

CHAPTER II.

This chapter on the *geography* of the Abbey, as I call it, has nothing to do with the stories which begin in the next chapter, and the only reason that I have written it at all is this. In the days when I first heard many of the stories which I am going to tell you now, they were told to us by Dean Stanley in the Abbey. As we walked about with him he explained to us what part of the church we were in, and pointed out the tomb or monument of the man, or woman, or child about whom he was telling us. But some of you may read this little book before you have ever been to Westminster Abbey, and others may have been there, but may not know the names of the different parts of the church, or where any particular monument or tomb is.

So, instead of trying to explain at the beginning of every story whereabouts we are supposed to be standing, I am putting all such explanations in this chapter; and this will, I hope, help you to find your way about in the Abbey for yourselves. If you only want to hear the stories, you must miss this chapter and go on to the next one.

Just as we have maps to understand the geography of countries, so we have maps, which are called *plans*, to understand the geography of churches and houses, and the drawing you see on the opposite page is a map or plan of the inside of Westminster Abbey. The picture at the beginning of this book is a view of the outside.

We will now suppose we have just come into the Abbey at the great west door, the door between the two towers (see frontispiece). The name is marked on the plan.* We should

---

* The west door is hardly ever used now as an entrance for visitors, and if we were really coming to the Abbey we should

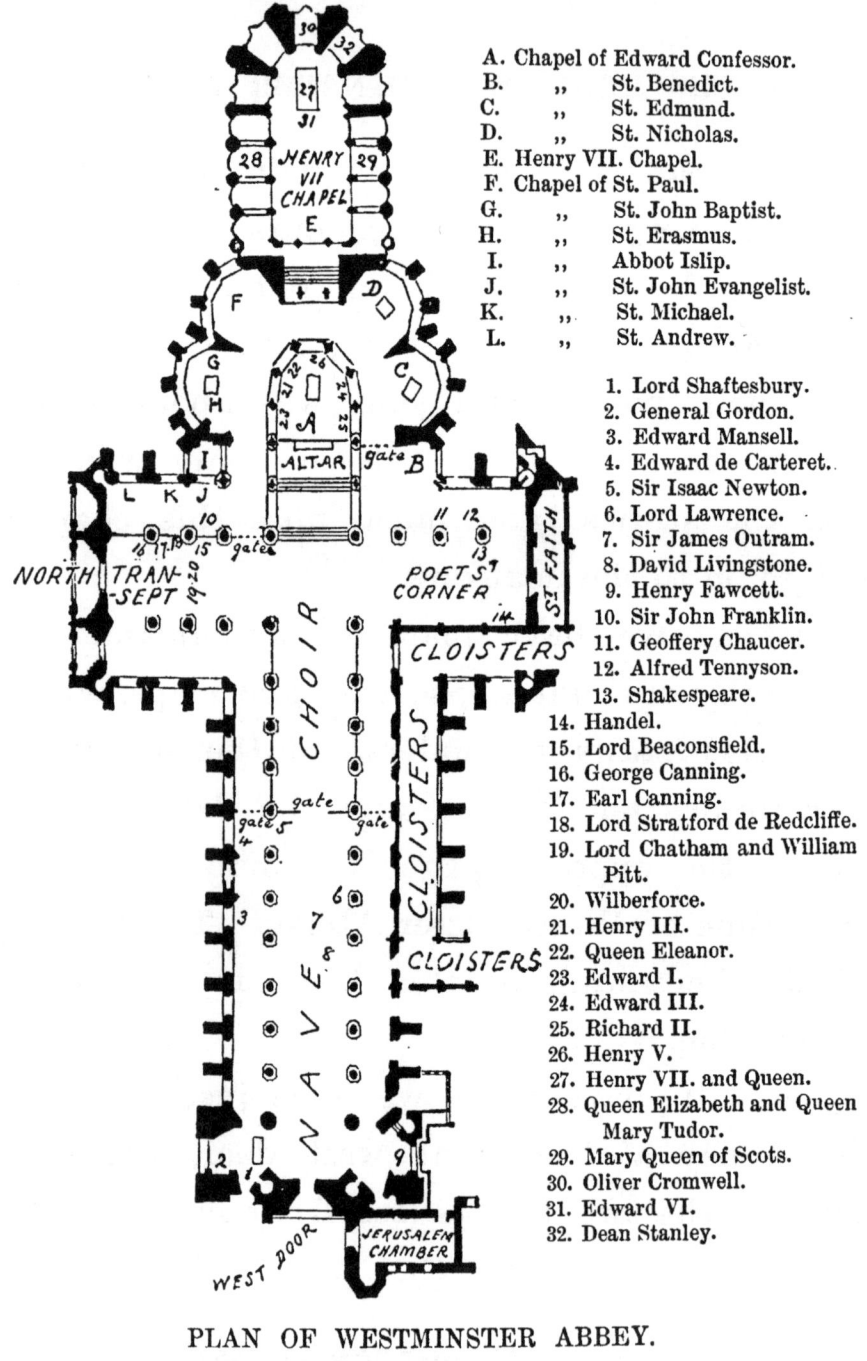

PLAN OF WESTMINSTER ABBEY.

Scale of 5 100 feet.

[*To face p.* 14.

then be standing in what is called the nave, and right in front of us and through those iron gates underneath the organ is the choir. That is where service is held every morning and every afternoon, and where all the Westminster School boys sit on Sundays when they come to church, for as Westminster school has no chapel of its own, the boys have all their services in the Abbey. Through the choir gates you can see the communion table in front of you, and behind that, again, are all the chapels where the kings and queens are buried. The nave and transepts are full of the monuments and graves of great men. The numbers 1, 2, 3, etc., on the plan mark those about which you will find stories later on.

And now, if you look at the plan, you will see exactly where everything is. The

enter by another door, called Solomon's Porch, close by St. Margaret's Church. But as soon as we had got inside we should walk straight down to the great west door, and imagine we had just come in that way.

whole Abbey is built on a piece of land which has the shape of a cross laid upon the ground. The nave and choir represent the stem of the cross, and the two transepts form the two arms.

In the part of the choir beyond the communion table are the chapels. Altogether there are eleven, and they are arranged like a wreath round the shrine of Edward the Confessor. They are marked on the plan by the letters A, B, C, etc., and their names you will find on the plan, beginning with A, which is the Chapel of Edward the Confessor.

One last thing I must explain before we begin the stories, and that is—how this great church came to be called an Abbey, and not a Cathedral. It is not at all difficult to remember when you have once been told.

The Church of St. Peter did not stand, as you may have supposed, all by itself on Thorney Isle, but was only one part of a mass of buildings called the Monastery of St. Peter.

A monastery, as you very likely already know, was a kind of college for monks. Here they lived under the rule of an abbot; and the church belonging to the monastery—for every monastery had a church, as well as a school and hospital or infirmary, belonging to it—was called an Abbey.

In early days the life of the monks was a very busy one. They did all the rough work, such as cooking, and cleaning pots and pans; for although many of them had been great soldiers or great nobles, they did not think any work done for the monastery was beneath them. They ploughed the land and planted seeds; they cut down trees for firewood; they nursed the sick; they fed and looked after the poor who lived round about them; and they taught in the school, and watched over the boys who were sent there to be educated.

Many boys—not only those who intended to become monks when they grew up, but those also who were to go out into the world, or become soldiers—went to the monastery schools to be taught. Here the sons of great nobles sat to learn their lessons side by side with the children of the poorest people, who were allowed to come and have as good an education as the rich without paying any school fees. The schools were open to all who wished to learn.

Of course, Scripture was the chief thing that they were taught, but the monks did not think that alone was enough, and the boys often learnt, besides reading and writing, grammar, poetry, astronomy, and arithmetic. Latin many of the monks talked almost as easily as their own language, and very often music and painting were added to all this. In the cloisters, or covered walks belonging to the monastery, the boys learned their lessons, always with a master near by, and sitting one behind another, so that no signals or jokes were possible. And very hard it must have been to keep their attention on their work in summer time when, if they looked up, they could see through the open archways the sun shining on the grass in the centre of the cloisters, and inviting them to come and play there. Something was always going on in the cloisters. Sometimes the school-boys were tempted to waste their time watching the monks shaving. Once a fortnight in summer, and once in three weeks in winter, the monks came out here with hot water and soap, and the important business of shaving went on, while on "Saturdays the heads and feet of the brethren were duly washed." If while all these things were going on the abbot appeared, every one stood up and bowed, and the lessons and the shaving and the washing stopped until he had passed by.

Perhaps the most important part of every monastery was the library, and an abbot who cared much for the monastery over which he ruled tried to collect and preserve and buy as many books as he could. In those days printing was not invented, and so every book of which many copies were wanted had to be written out by the monks. And this they did in a most wonderful way, copying them, so we are told,* "on parchment of extreme fineness prepared by their own hands," and ornamenting them with "the most delicate miniatures and paintings." The monks at that time loved their books more than anything else, and there was a saying among them that a cloister without books was like a fortress without an arsenal. Often they took long and difficult journeys to see or to copy the books in other monasteries. "Our books," said a monk, "are our delight and our wealth in time of peace, . . . our food when we are hungry, and our medicine when we are sick."

And now, having told you a little about the life of the monks in those far-off days, we must come back to these buildings on Thorney Isle, which as I have said were called the Monastery of St. Peter. It is not known when this particular monastery was first founded; but it is said that

* Montalembert, "Monks of the West."

St. Dunstan, who lived in the reign of King Edwy, found there some half-ruined buildings. He repaired them, and then brought twelve monks to live in company with him. But probably the Danes, who were often invading England at that time, destroyed this little monastery, for when Edward the Confessor came to the throne, many years afterwards, it had almost, if not quite, disappeared; and when he rebuilt it he added this great church of St. Peter, about which I told you in the first chapter.

There is a pretty story told of how this came about. An old monk was one day lying asleep, and in his sleep he was commanded by St. Peter, who appeared visibly to him, to acquaint the king that it was his pleasure he should restore the monastery. "There is," said the apostle, "a place of mine in the west part of London which I choose and love. The name of the place is Thorney. . . . There let the king by my command make a dwelling of monks, stately build and amply endow; it shall be no less than the House of God, and the Gates of Heaven." When he woke up, the old monk went to the king and told him his vision. Upon hearing it Edward journeyed to "the west part of London;" there he found Thorney Isle, and there he built the monastery and church, which he called after the apostle.

And now at last we have finished all the explanations. In the first chapter I told you how the Abbey came to be built, and in this one I have shown you how to find your way about it. In the next I shall begin telling you the stories, the first being about Lord Shaftesbury, whose monument is in the nave, where you see No. 1 on the plan.

CHAPTER III.

Very likely you have never even heard the name of Lord Shaftesbury; but as you will be sure to read and hear of him by-and-by, I will tell you a little about what he did, and why a monument was put up in his memory. He was born in 1801, and died in 1885, and so was an old man of eighty-four when he died. He spent all his long life in trying to make other people—especially the poorest and most miserable he could find—more happy and more comfortable. He was a great nobleman, and very rich, and he gave most of his time to finding out the cause of the suffering of the poorest people in England, and, when he had found it out, he helped to make laws to improve things for them, and, if money was wanted, he gave that too. But he gave away his money wisely and well; he never was taken in by idle people and beggars who would not work for themselves; his motto seems to have been to "help those who help themselves," and one name by which he was known was "The Working Man's Friend." But especially may he be remembered by all children for what he did for children. More than fifty years ago, when first machines (spinning machines and weaving machines) were invented in the great cotton factories in England, it was found that children could work them just as well as men and women; and as children would not have to be paid so much as men, the masters of the mills began to employ them. Quite tiny children, sometimes not more than five years old, and so small that they often had to be lifted up on stools to reach their work, were made to toil in the mills and factories all day, and sometimes all night too. They were treated like little slaves. If they did not work fast enough, they were beaten and kicked by their masters; and they spent all their days in hot rooms, hearing nothing but the whirring of the machines, and stopping their work only for about half an hour in the middle of the day for their dinner, which was generally only black bread and porridge, and sometimes a little bacon. They had no time for play, and they had no time to rest, except on Sundays, and then they were too tired to move from the berths (or shelves) where they slept, for they did not even have proper beds.

Then, again, there were the children who worked in coal-mines, who spent all their days in damp, dark mines, who never saw the sun, and who had to draw the trucks filled with coal, or carry great baskets full of it on their backs. And all this they began to do before they were six years old.

When Lord Shaftesbury saw these things—for he went into the mills and the factories, and he went down into the mines—he made up his mind that something must be done for such children. So he made speeches in Parliament, in which he told of the cruelty with which thousands of English children were treated; and at last laws were made by which it was forbidden to let such little children work in mines and factories at all, and by which older children were given shorter hours to work and more time for rest and fresh air. All this and much more Lord Shaftesbury did during his long life, and when at last he died, this monument was put up in Westminster Abbey with these words on it, so that people who had never known him might be always reminded of the way he spent his life:—

LORD SHAFTESBURY,
BORN 1801; DIED 1885.
ENDEARED TO HIS COUNTRYMEN BY A LONG LIFE SPENT IN THE CAUSE OF THE HELPLESS AND SUFFERING.
" LOVE—SERVE."

Close to Lord Shaftesbury, there is a monument to a great soldier, General Gordon,* who was killed in Egypt in 1885—the same year that Lord Shaftesbury died. He fought in the Crimean War and in China, and was often called "Chinese Gordon." All the soldiers who served under him were so fond and proud of him that they would have done anything for him. He was very brave, and it was well known that he would always be in the front rank to lead his men when there was a battle, and this, more than anything else, made him popular. He himself never was armed except with a little cane, which his soldiers called "the wand of victory." Once when he was wounded his men wanted to carry him out of the battle, but he would not allow it, and went on leading them till he fainted from pain and weakness.

Lord Shaftesbury, the great statesman, died in England, with all his many friends near him, and General Gordon, the great soldier, was

* No. 2 on plan.

killed by savages while he was shut up in Khartoum, a town in Africa, where he was besieged; but their two monuments are close together in Westminster Abbey, and they were alike in one thing—they both did all they could to help other people. Of course, Gordon had not time to do so much as Lord Shaftesbury,* but when he was not fighting he lived in England, and then "his house," said a gentleman who knew him,† "was school and hospital and almshouse in turn. The poor, the sick, and the unfortunate were all welcome. He always took a great delight in children, but especially in boys employed on the river or the sea. Many he rescued from the gutter, cleansed them and clothed them, and kept them for weeks in his house. For their benefit he established reading classes. He called them his kings, and for many of them he got berths on board ship. One day a friend asked him why there were so

---

* Gordon was fifty-two when he was killed.
† See Mr. Hake's "Life of Gordon."

many pins stuck into the map of the world over his mantelpiece. He was told they marked and followed the course of the boys on their voyages; that they were moved from point to point as his youngsters advanced, and that he prayed for them as they went night and day. The light in which he was held by those lads was shown by inscriptions in chalk on the fences. A favourite one was 'God bless the Kernel,'" which was their way of spelling "colonel," for he was at that time Colonel Gordon.

But I must not stay to tell you more of him now, for there are many other people I want you to hear about. "This Abbey," Dean Stanley used to say, "is full of the remembrances of great men and famous women. But it is also full of the remembrances of little boys and girls whose death shot a pang through the hearts of those who loved them, and who wished that they should never be forgotten."

So now, not far from the monuments to these two great men, we come upon the tombs of two boys who are buried here: one Edward Mansell,* a boy of fourteen, who died as long ago as 1681; and another Edward, Edward de Carteret,† a little boy "seven yeares and nine months old," who "dyed the 30th day of October, 1677." His father and mother put nothing on his tomb to tell us about him except that he was a "gentleman;" but that one word tells us much, for it means, said Dean Stanley, that "they believed—and no belief can be so welcome to any father or mother—they believed that their little son was growing up truthful, manly, courageous, courteous, unselfish, and religious." And if this little boy had tried to be a "gentleman" in this true and best sense of the word, it does not seem out of place that he should be buried in the Abbey among great men and famous women.

Close by little Edward de Carteret is buried Sir Isaac Newton.‡ There is on the floor a plain grey stone with these few words in Latin on it, "Hic depositum quod mortale fuit Isaaci

* No. 3 on plan. † No. 4 on plan. ‡ No. 5 on plan.

Newtoni," which means, "Here lies what was mortal of Isaac Newton." Sir Isaac Newton was one of the most celebrated Englishmen who ever lived, and made wonderful discoveries in science, especially in astronomy, by which his name is known all over the world. He was born on Christmas Day, 1642, and lived to be seventy-five years old. In spite of being so learned and so famous, he was always modest about what he knew, and believed that what he had learned and discovered was only a very, very little bit of all there was to learn and discover in the world and about the world. When he was quite an old man, some one was saying to him one day how much he had done and how wonderful his discoveries were, and he answered, "To myself I seem to have been as a child picking up shells on the seashore, while the great ocean of truth lay unexplored before me."

Just above the grey stone in the floor there is a large statue of Sir Isaac Newton, sitting with his head resting on his hands as though he were thinking, and a great pile of books by his side.

I have already told you about General Gordon. I now come to the story of another great soldier, Sir James Outram, who is buried in the Abbey. The graves of Sir James Outram and of David Livingstone, a great traveller and missionary, and of Lord Lawrence, who was the Governor-General of India, and who did a great deal for the natives while he lived among them, are all close together, and there is something interesting to tell you about all these three men, especially Sir James Outram and David Livingstone.

If you have read or heard anything of the story of the Indian Mutiny, when the native soldiers of India rebelled against the English who governed them, and killed hundreds of men, women, and children, you must, I think, have heard the names of Lord Lawrence and Sir James Outram.

During the years he had lived among them, the natives of India had grown so fond of Lord

Lawrence,* that when the mutiny (or rebellion) broke out, the men of the Punjaub (which was the part of India he then governed) said they would be true to the man who had been good to them, and so they fought for England with the few English soldiers who were then in India, and helped us to conquer the rebels. Lord Lawrence has been called the "Saviour of India," because he came to the help of his fellow-countrymen with these Indian soldiers just when he was most terribly needed.

Later on, in the same war, came the siege of Lucknow. Lucknow was one of the chief cities of India, but the streets were long and narrow and dirty, and most of the houses were poor and mean. Among them, however, were some magnificent palaces and temples. The Residency, the house where the English governor of Lucknow lived, was built on a hill above the river, and all round it were the offices and the bungalows of the English who were living there.

* No. 6 on plan.

C

When the mutiny broke out, it was soon seen that the native soldiers would attack the English in Lucknow, and the people at once set to work to make as many preparations against them as they could. To begin with, Sir Henry Lawrence, who was in command of the soldiers both English and Indian, and who was the brother of Lord Lawrence, of whom we spoke just now, ordered all the women and children to come and live in the Residency, which was supposed to be the safest place in Lucknow. Then guns, powder and shot, and food were brought in and stored in the cellars. At last, at nine o'clock on the evening of the 30th of May, 1857, when the officers were quietly at dinner, nearly all the native soldiers in Lucknow suddenly rose against the English. They loaded their guns, and fired at every one they could see; they broke into the houses, and, after stealing everything they could, set fire to them; and all night there was nothing to be heard save the savage yells of the rebels and the firing of the guns, and nothing to be seen but fighting men and burning houses. About five hundred of the native soldiers were true to the English, and they stayed with them and fought against their rebellious countrymen through all the long siege of Lucknow. For though the rebels were beaten at their first rising by the English, yet in a month or two they rose again, and then every one, including the soldiers, was driven by the enemy into the Residency, which was the last place of refuge.

Some day, perhaps, you will read a poem by Lord Tennyson called "Lucknow," which describes all the terrible things that happened during the "eighty-seven" days the English and the faithful natives were shut up in the Residency, on the topmost roof of which, as he says, the "banner of England blew" during the whole siege, though it was shot through by bullets, and torn and tattered, and faded in the hot Indian summer sun.

One of the first things that happened was

that Sir Henry Lawrence was killed. He was lying on his bed one morning talking to an officer, when a shell was fired from a cannon into his room. It burst as it fell, and some of its fragments wounded Sir Henry so terribly that he died the next day. Almost the last thing he said to the other officers was to beg them never to give in to the natives, but to fight as long as there was an English man left alive. Lord Lawrence, his brother, who died some years afterwards, was buried, as you remember, in Westminster Abbey; but Sir Henry Lawrence was carried out of the Residency while the fighting was going on, and the bullets were falling like rain, and buried side by side with some private soldiers who had also been killed by the rebels. On his gravestone they put these words, which he himself had asked should be written there, "Here lies Henry Lawrence, who tried to do his duty."

This was on the 4th of July, and Sir Henry Lawrence had said he thought it would be possible to defend the Residency for a fortnight. But as time went on the English grew fewer and fewer; every day more soldiers were killed, and every day many died of their wounds, while those who were left alive had to fight day and night. The English ladies nursed the sick men, and cooked the food, which they used to bring out to those who were fighting; and they looked after the children, very many of whom died too. For it was the hottest time of the year in India—a time when English children are sent away to the hills to get fresh air—and, besides suffering from the heat, they missed all the comforts they were accustomed to; they had no milk and very little to eat, and they were terrified by the noise of the firing and all the confusion.

But still the fighting went on day after day, long after the fortnight was over, and day after day the enemy saw the English flag still flying on the roof of the Residency, and began to think they never would conquer this brave little band of Englishmen.

All this time, however, though they did not know it in the Residency, Sir James Outram* and Sir Henry Havelock, with more English soldiers, were fighting their way to Lucknow.†

They had both been for many years in India, and were two of the bravest and best men who could possibly have been sent to the relief of the little band who had been besieged for so many weeks. On the 23rd of September, nearly *twelve weeks* after the day Sir Henry Lawrence died, it was heard in Lucknow that Sir James Outram and Sir Henry Havelock were close by, and on the 25th the Highlanders were in the city and fighting their way through the narrow streets to the Residency. Then from every window and every balcony and every roof the rebels fired down on them. Many were killed and more were wounded. A story is

* No. 7 on plan.

† Sir James Outram was born on the 29th of January, 1805, and Sir Henry Havelock was born on the 5th of April, 1795; so at the time of the siege of Lucknow Sir James was fifty-one, and Sir Henry sixty-two years old.

told, by Mr. Archibald Forbes,* of two Irishmen who were in the Highland regiment. "They were great friends, named Glandell and M'Donough, and in going through one of these narrow streets M'Donough's leg was broken by a bullet. He fell, but he was not left to die, for his friend who was by him took him on his back and trudged on with his heavy burden. Although he was carrying M'Donough, Glandell determined to fight at the same time, so when there was a chance to fire a shot, he propped his wounded comrade up against a wall and took up his rifle instead; then he would pick up M'Donough again and stagger cheerily on till a place of safety was reached."

At last the gate of the Residency was in sight of the relieving force, and then the besieged people looking out saw through the smoke officers on horseback—Outram with a great cut across his face, and one arm in a sling, on a big white horse, and Havelock walking by his

* See "Havelock," by Archibald Forbes ("English Men of Action Series").

side (for his horse had been shot), and the Highlanders in their kilts and for the most part in their shirt-sleeves, with no coats on. "Then," wrote some one who had been all these weeks in the Residency—"then all our doubts and fears were over, and from every pit, trench, and battery, from behind the sand-bags piled on shattered houses, from every post still held by a few gallant spirits, even from the hospital, rose cheer on cheer." Sir James Outram's horse shied at the gate, but with a shout the Highlanders hoisted him through; Sir Henry Havelock followed, "and then in rushed the eager soldiers, powder-grimed, dusty, and bloody, . . and all round them as they swarmed in crowded . . the fighting men of the garrison, and the civilians whom the siege had made into soldiers, and women weeping tears of joy, and the sick and the wounded who had crawled out of the hospital to welcome their deliverers. The ladies came down among the soldiers to shake their hands, and the children hugged them." "We were all rushing about," said a lady, "to give the poor fellows drinks of water, for they were perfectly exhausted; and tea was made, of which a large party of tired, thirsty officers partook without milk and sugar, and we had nothing to give them to eat. Every one's tongue seemed going at once with so much to ask and to tell, and the faces of utter strangers beamed on each other like those of dearest friends and brothers." So ended the siege of Lucknow. Sir Henry Havelock had not been wounded, but he had suffered much from hard work and from having so little to eat. "I find it not so easy to starve at sixty as at forty-seven," he said one day. At last, in November, he became very ill, and when Sir James Outram went to see him in the common soldier's tent which he had always used since he had been in Lucknow, he told him that he was going to die; "but I have for forty years so ruled my life that when death came I might face it without fear," he added.

He died on the 24th of November, 1857, and was buried just outside Lucknow, under a mango tree, and even now the letter H, which was carved in the bark—for no other monument could be put up to his memory in those days of war and disturbance—can just be seen, more than thirty years afterwards.

Sir James Outram was nursed in Dr. Fayrer's house in Lucknow until he was well, and three years afterwards, in 1860, he left India and came back to England. Then he had many honours shown him; but, like Sir Henry Havelock, he felt the effects of all he had gone through in India, and gradually he became more ill, and was at last sent to the south of France, where he died on the 11th of March, 1863. His body was brought to England and buried in the Abbey under the grey stone which you will see in the nave, and on it were written these words—

LIEUTENANT-GENERAL SIR JAMES OUTRAM,
BORN JAN. 29TH, 1805; DIED MAR. 11TH, 1863.
"THE BAYARD OF INDIA."

I remember, in one of the sermons which he used to preach to children, Dean Stanley spoke of this grave of Sir James Outram, and said, "There was a famous French soldier of bygone days whose name you will see written in this Abbey on the gravestone of Sir James Outram, because in many ways he was like Bayard. Bayard was a small boy—only thirteen—when he went into his first service, and his mother told him to remember three things : first, to fear and love God; secondly, to have gentle and courteous manners to those above him; and thirdly, to be generous and charitable, without pride or haughtiness, to those beneath him; and these three things he never forgot, which helped to make him the soldier without fear and without reproach." And it was in these three things that Sir James Outram was supposed to be so like the French soldier, Bayard.

One more thing I must tell you before we pass on to David Livingstone. On the morning of the day when Outram was to be buried, some

44 TALES FROM WESTMINSTER ABBEY.

Highland soldiers came to his house and asked to be allowed to carry the coffin on their shoulders down to the Abbey. They were some men from the 78th Regiment—the very same men who had fought under him at the relief of Lucknow, and who had been with him when Sir Henry Havelock was buried under the mango tree; and they came now hoping to carry the body of Sir James Outram to his burial. Unfortunately, they were too late, and were told, much to their disappointment, that this was impossible because other arrangements had been made.

We come now to David Livingstone,* the great traveller and missionary. He was born in Scotland in 1813. His father and mother were very poor, and when he was ten years old he was sent to work in a cotton factory. He grew up to be a very extraordinary man, as you will see, and he certainly was a very unusual boy. He saved up his wages, and the first thing

* No. 8 on plan.

he bought was a Latin grammar, from which he used to learn in the evenings after he left his work; and so interested was he that he often went on till twelve o'clock at night, when his mother took away the book and sent him to bed, for he had to be at the factory at six every morning. When he grew up he became a missionary, and went to Africa, where he made many discoveries, travelling into parts of the country where no one had ever been before, and teaching the natives, who were quite ignorant and wild, but who grew very fond of this "white man who treated black men as his brothers"—for so one native chief described him—and who cared for them, and doctored them when they were ill, and gave up all his life to them. He had all sorts of adventures. Once he lived for some time in a place which was full of lions, who used to come and kill the cattle even in the day time. The people made up their minds to try to kill one lion; for if one of a party of lions is killed, the rest generally go away. Livingstone went out with them, and they found the lions on a little hill covered with trees. Some of the men fired, but did not hit any of them. Presently Livingstone "saw one of the beasts sitting on a rock, behind a little bush"—these are his own words—"about thirty yards off. I took a good aim at his body through the bush, and fired at him. The men then called out, 'He is shot—he is shot!' others cried out, 'He has been shot by another man, too; let us go to him.' I did not see any one else shoot at him, but I saw the lion's tail erected in anger behind the bush, and, turning to the people, said, 'Stop a little till I fire again.' When in the act of ramming down the bullets I heard a shout. Starting and looking half round, I saw the lion in the act of springing on me. I was upon a little height. He caught my shoulder as he sprang, and we both came to the ground together. Growling horribly close to my ear, he shook me as a terrier dog does a rat." It was wonderful that Livingstone did not seem to feel any pain or fear; he said he seemed to be in a kind of dream, but knew quite well all that was happening. Of course, in another minute he would have been killed, had not some of the people fired again at the lion and this time killed it. But Livingstone never afterwards could use quite easily the arm which the lion had crushed. During his travels he discovered Lake Nyassa, which you can find marked now on every map of Africa. Before he went there all that part of the country used to be marked "unexplored."

For more than thirty years Livingstone lived in Africa, always travelling about, and finding new tribes of natives, all of whom he got to know, and all of whom became fond of him; and at last, when he died in a little hut which his black servants had built for him in the middle of one of these great African forests, Susi and Chumah, two of his followers, who had been with him for many years, came all the way to England with the body of their dead master. On the day when he was buried, the Abbey was crowded with people who came from all parts of England and Scotland; and among all the white faces were seen two black ones, for the faithful servants stood close by the grave; and Dean Stanley, who read the service, said afterwards that he had never seen two men seem more broken-hearted. On his tombstone you will read of one more thing which he did for the natives whilst he lived among them; and that was, to help to abolish the slave-trade in Central Africa. He was sixty years old when he died, and he had worked all his life to raise the lives of thousands of African savages into something better and happier.

Many other great men I have no time to tell you about, but there are two more, of whom I particularly want you to hear a few words—Henry Fawcett and Sir John Franklin. Henry Fawcett* was not a soldier, nor a great

* No. 9 on plan.

traveller, but he was known for many years all over England as the "Blind Postmaster-General." He was not born blind, and why I want to tell you about him is to show you what a brave man can do when such a terrible misfortune as becoming blind happens to him. He was born in 1833, and died in 1884, and for twenty-six years of his life he was quite blind. He lost his sight in this way. He was out shooting one day with his father, who fired at a bird without noticing that his son was close by. Suddenly he saw that some of the shots, instead of hitting the bird, had hit his son in the eyes. Henry Fawcett was wearing spectacles, and a shot went through each of the glasses, making a little round hole in them, and then going on into his eyes. From that moment he never saw again. His first thought, he afterwards told his sister, was that he should never again see the lovely view, and the colours of the autumn leaves on the trees, as he had seen them a moment before; his second thought was to try and do everything he could to comfort his father, who must need comfort almost as much as he did himself. So, at twenty-five years of age, Henry Fawcett, who had made up his mind to work hard as a barrister—for he was very poor—and make enough money to go into Parliament, which had been his great wish ever since he was at school, suddenly found all his plans and all his hopes upset. But his courage never gave way; he determined that his blindness should not make him a helpless, disappointed man. "In ten minutes after the accident," he said some years later, "he had made up his mind that he would stick to what he had meant to do." And so he did. He had been a great rider, a great skater, and a great fisherman, and all these things he kept up. He skated with his friends, holding on to a stick by which they guided him; he rode, he fished, he walked, behaving in all things as though he were not blind. He was obliged to give up being a barrister, but he became a professor at Cambridge. He wrote in papers and magazines (of course some one had to do the actual writing for him, but he dictated it), and at last, when he was thirty-two years old, that is to say, seven years after the accident, he achieved his object, and became member of Parliament (the Blind Member, he was sometimes called) for Brighton.

It would take too long to tell you of all the work he did for his country after he was in Parliament, but he was always trying to improve things; he was never idle, and at last, when he was made Postmaster-General, he hardly ever had time for a holiday. He was a favourite with every one, and, when he was ill, telegrams and letters used to come from all parts of England to ask after him. He always took a great interest in other blind people, and was fond of saying to them, "Do what you can to act as though you were not blind; be of good courage, and help yourselves." And to his friends, and all who had blind friends or relations, he was never tired of saying, "Do not treat us as though you pitied us for our misfortune; the kindest thing that can be done or said to a blind person is to help him as far as possible to be of good cheer, to give him confidence that help will be afforded him whenever necessary, that there is still good work for him to do, and, the more active his career, the more useful his life to others, the more happy his days to himself." These are his own words. They are brave words; but Henry Fawcett was, as you have seen, a brave man, and fought and conquered all the great difficulties with which his blindness surrounded him, with as much courage as Sir James Outram showed when he fought his way into Lucknow, or David Livingstone when he journeyed through the deserts and forests of Africa. And that is why a memorial of him was put up in Westminster Abbey by the people of England, who subscribed for it, so that the heroic life of the Blind Postmaster-General should never be forgotten.

Sir John Franklin* was a sailor and a great Arctic explorer, who made many expeditions, and went nearer to the North Pole than any man had ever been before. He and his companions endured every kind of hardship in the ice and the snow of the Arctic regions. He died on his third expedition, just two years after last leaving England, and was buried in the far-away cold North amidst the snow under slabs of ice. On the monument in Westminster Abbey, which was put up in his memory by his wife, Lady Franklin, are written the words "O ye frost and cold, O ye ice and snow, bless ye the Lord: praise Him, and magnify Him for ever." The story of the expedition is a very sad one, for, during the winter after Sir John's death, it became clear to the sailors that the ships were so fast in the ice, which

* No. 10 on plan.

had closed in and frozen all round them, that they would never be able to move again. So at last, nearly all the provisions being exhausted, the men abandoned their ships, and with boats and sledges, which they carried or dragged over the ice, set out to walk southwards in the hope that they might at last reach the unfrozen sea and meet a ship. But this they never did, for they were starved and ill, and although another expedition had been sent from England to look for them, it was too late to save them. The only traces ever found of them were their skeletons, and the boats and sledges, containing many books and papers which Sir John had written, saying how far he had been, and what he had done on this voyage from which he never returned.

His epitaph, written by Lord Tennyson, is one of the most beautiful in the Abbey —

"Not here! the white North has thy bones; and thou,
   Heroic sailor-soul,
Art passing on thine happier voyage now
   Toward no earthly pole."

CHAPTER IV.

IN Westminster Abbey are the graves of many poets—so many that one part of the church (the south transept) is always known as Poets' Corner.

Geoffrey Chaucer,* who wrote among other things a book called the "Canterbury Tales," and who died as long ago as 1400, was one of the first English poets buried in Poets' Corner; and the last was Alfred Tennyson,† who died in 1892, and was buried close beside Chaucer, just four hundred and ninety-two years afterwards.

When I was telling you the story of the Indian Mutiny, I spoke of a poem called "Lucknow," which described in a wonderful way the sufferings of the people who were shut up in the Residency during the long siege.

* No. 11 on plan. † No. 12 on plan.

This poem and very many others were written by Alfred Tennyson, the great poet, who was made by the Queen Poet Laureate of England, and then, many years afterwards, Lord Tennyson, by which name you will always hear him spoken of.

There is a story told of how the first verses Alfred Tennyson ever made were written. His father was a clergyman, and Alfred and his brothers and sisters lived all their lives in the country, running wild in the woods and the fields, and learning all about birds and flowers, until they were old enough to go to school. One Sunday morning, when every one but Alfred, who was then very small, was going to church, his elder brother Charles said he would give him something to do, and told him he must write some verses about the flowers in the garden. When they came in, Alfred appeared with his slate covered all over with his first poem. He was very fond of story-telling, and he and his brothers and sisters would combine to make up long and exciting tales which sometimes lasted for months. When he went to school he began to read a great deal, especially poetry. If he found any he particularly liked, he would try to imitate it in poems of his own, and in this way he and his brother Charles, who was with him at school, used to spend a great deal of their spare time.

It would take too long, and it would not be interesting, to tell you the names of even the chief poems which Lord Tennyson wrote. By-and-by you will read many of them for yourselves, and two I am sure you will specially enjoy. One is the "Siege of Lucknow," which we have so often spoken of; and the other is the "Revenge," which is also a story of fighting —but a sea-fight in the time of Queen Elizabeth. Lord Tennyson, like most poets, was more fond of the country than of towns, and most of his life he lived either in the Isle of Wight or in Surrey. He used, until quite the end of his life, to enjoy taking long country walks, and he never lost his love for flowers or birds, or failed to notice them; and this in spite of having all his life been very short-sighted. It was said of him that "when he was looking at any object he seemed to be smelling it," so closely used he to hold it to his eyes.

And yet, with this difficulty, he noticed "more than most men with perfect sight would see. I remember his telling me," so wrote a friend of his, "*if you tread on daisies they turn up underfoot and get rosy.* His hearing, on the other hand, was exceptionally keen, and he held it as a sort of compensation for his blurred sight; he could hear *the shriek of a bat*, which he always said was the test of a quick ear."

Lord Tennyson was eighty-three when he died, and when he was buried in Westminster Abbey the great church was crowded, not only during the funeral service, but for many days and even weeks afterwards, by hundreds of people, who came to see, and lay flowers on, his grave.

Although so many poets were buried in the Abbey, yet there were many others who when they died were buried in the country, or in other churches in London, and, when this was the case, monuments were often put up in the Abbey in memory of them. For instance, Shakespeare,* the greatest of all our great poets, was buried at Stratford-on-Avon, where he had lived for the last part of his life, and where he died.

There is not a very great deal known about his life. He was the son of a country shopkeeper, who was very poor, but who managed to send his son to the grammar school at Stratford-on-Avon, where they lived. When he was fourteen he was taken away from school, and had to earn his own living. It is sometimes said that he was first a butcher's boy, and had to carry out the meat, but no one knows exactly what he did after he left school until he was about nineteen. Then he went to London, and began to write poetry and plays.

* No. 13 on plan.

He had at this time hardly any money, and was thankful to earn a penny whenever he could by holding horses, or making himself useful in any way he could think of, and was nicknamed by his friends "Jack-of-all-trades." At last he got employment as a writer of plays for the Globe Theatre. This Globe Theatre was very different from the theatres of nowadays. It was a round wooden building with no roof, except just over the stage, and there it was covered in to protect the dresses of the actors and actresses in case of bad weather. Gradually it became clear that this William Shakespeare, who had come to London quite a poor and unknown man, was a great poet, his plays began to be talked of, and many great and rich men became his friends. In a few years he was no longer poor, and had begun to save money to buy himself a house at Stratford-on-Avon, where he had been born. To do this had always been a dream of his: for a long time his wife and children had been living there while he worked hard for them in London, and when at last he had bought his house, which was called New Place, he left London and went home to them.

Many years passed away, and Shakespeare, who had written great plays such as *Hamlet* and *The Merchant of Venice*, which you will all know and perhaps see acted some day, lived quietly in the little town of Stratford-on-Avon, making friends of all the people round him, both rich and poor, and seeing his own plays acted in a great empty barn near his house, for in those days there was no theatre in Stratford.

"Master Shakespeare," as he was called, was buried in the churchyard of the little town he had been so fond of all his life; and many years afterwards, when his name had become known all over England, and his plays and his poems had become famous as they had never been during his lifetime, a monument was put up to his memory in Westminster Abbey close by the graves of two other poets, Spenser and Drayton, who had been his friends: on it are written these words out of his own play of *The Tempest*—

> " The Cloud-capt Towers,
> The Gorgeous Palaces,
> The Solemn Temples,
> The Great Globe itself,
> Yea, all which it inherit,
> Shall dissolve;
> And, like the baseless fabric of a vision,
> Leave not a wreck behind." *

Among all the poets who are buried in the south transept, there is one great musician, George Frederick Handel.† Dean Stanley says that "Handel, who composed the music of the 'Messiah' and the 'Israel in Egypt,' must have been a poet no less than a musician, and therefore he was not unfitly buried in Poets' Corner."

Handel was the son of a German doctor, and was born in a little German town. As a boy he was very fond of music, but as his father

* This is the actual inscription on the monument. The last line as written by Shakespeare reads, "Leave not a rack behind."

† No. 14 on plan.

meant him to be a lawyer, he would not let him hear any for fear that he would want to be a musician. Once,* when George was seven years old, his father went to visit another son who lived at the court of the Duke of Saxe-Weissenfels. The little boy, who had most likely heard his brother speak of the court concerts, begged to go too, but of course he was told that it was impossible. His father drove off, but still George determined to go. He managed to slip out, and ran as long as he could after the carriage. At last he was seen and taken in, and as there was no time to bring him home, he went with his father to the court. He soon made friends among the duke's musicians, who let him try the organ. One day after the service he was lifted on to the organ-stool, and played so wonderfully that the duke, who was in church, asked who it was. When he heard that it was the little seven-year-old Handel, he sent for his father, and told

* See Sir George Grove's "Dictionary of Music."

him that his son would one day be such a great musician that it would be quite wrong to make him a lawyer. So from that day George was regularly taught music. When he was older he came to England, and here he lived most of his life, and here he wrote most of the music which is known almost all over the world. He used to give concerts at the English court, to which the Prince of Wales, the son of George II., and the princess, and many great people came. Sometimes at these concerts ladies would talk instead of listening to the music, and then Handel quite lost his temper. "His rage was uncontrollable," so we are told, "and sometimes carried him to the length of swearing and calling names; whereupon the gentle princess would say to the offenders, 'Hush, hush! Handel is angry;' and when all was quiet the concert would go on again." Handel, when he was old, became quite blind, but he still played the organ up to the very end of his life. He died on Good Friday, April 13, 1759, and was buried in the Abbey, and on his monument are written the words, "I know that my Redeemer liveth," from the Book of Job, which he had set to most beautiful music, and had asked to have written upon his tomb.

I have only spoken to you of Geoffrey Chaucer and of Alfred Tennyson, the first and the last poets who were buried in the Abbey; of Shakespeare, the greatest of all English poets, and of George Frederick Handel, the musician; but very many others are remembered in Poets' Corner. And when you some day walk round the Abbey you will see there the graves or monuments of most of the great English writers.

The north transept is full of the graves and monuments of statesmen. A great many of them you must have heard of, and some of you perhaps belong to the Primrose League, which was founded in 1881 in memory of Benjamin Disraeli,* Lord Beaconsfield, whose monument is in the Abbey. He was twice Prime Minister

* No. 15 on plan.

of England, and when he died the Primrose League (the badge of which is a primrose, and which was chosen because it was said to be his favourite flower) was started to band people together to carry on the work and help on the political party to which he had belonged. Then there are monuments to three members of one family—the family of Canning—who were all great statesmen. George Canning,* who was born as long ago as 1770, became known as a wonderful orator. When he was quite a small boy at school he used to say that he meant some day to be a member of Parliament, and at Eton he helped to start a debating society which was modelled on the House of Commons. Here his speeches soon became famous among the boys. He lived to be not only a member of Parliament, but Prime Minister of England. His youngest son Charles,† who was also a great man, became Earl Canning and first Viceroy of India.

* No. 16 on plan. † No. 17 on plan.

"The third great Canning" was Stratford Canning* (a cousin of Charles), who has been called "the greatest ambassador of our time," and who before he died was made Lord Stratford de Redcliffe, by which name he is best known. Each of these three great men gave all his time and all his strength to work for the good of his country. Two of them, George Canning and his son, the Viceroy of India, are buried in one grave here in the Abbey. Lord Stratford de Redcliffe, although his statue stands side by side with the monuments to his uncle and cousin, is buried in the little country churchyard of Frant, in Kent.

Lord Stratford de Redcliffe was an old man of ninety-three when he died. He had done so much, and known so many great and interesting people, that the story of his life is a book you will all like to read some day. One of the first things he remembered was how, when he was a little boy at school, he had seen Lord Nelson.

* No. 18 on plan.

It was at Eton, and Nelson, "with all his wounds and all his honours"—for so Lord Stratford describes him—came down to see the boys, and asked that they might have a whole holiday. More than eighty years afterwards, when Lord Stratford de Redcliffe died, there was found in his room a little picture of Lord Nelson, which he had kept ever since those far-off school days.

I remember Dean Stanley telling us that when Lord Stratford de Redcliffe was a very old man he remembered quite clearly what he had learnt and done when he was a little child at home. "Not long ago," the Dean said, "I was visiting this aged and famous statesman, and he repeated to me, word for word, the Evening Hymn beginning 'Glory to Thee, my God, this night,' as he had learnt it, he told me, from his nurse ninety years before."

I must not end this chapter without telling you the names of three more great statesmen. You will often hear the two Pitts and William

Wilberforce spoken of, and I should like to say a few words about all three before beginning the stories of the kings and queens.

William Pitt * was Prime Minister of England, and was made Lord Chatham by King George III. He and his son, the younger William Pitt,† are as well known to all Englishmen as George Canning and his son Earl Canning, about whom I have told you. Lord Chatham was, like George Canning, a great orator, and even when he was very old and very ill, he would come down to the Houses of Parliament and make wonderful speeches, which sometimes lasted as long as three hours and a half, but which were so interesting that they were listened to in perfect silence; "the stillness," it is said, "was so deep that the dropping of a handkerchief would have been heard." When he died he was buried in the Abbey; and in the same grave, twenty-eight years afterwards, was buried his son William, the second Pitt, who was an

* No. 19 on plan.   † Also No. 19 on plan.

even greater statesman than his father. This William was, when quite a little boy, astonishingly clever. "The fineness of William's mind," wrote his mother, in the old-fashioned words of those times, "makes him enjoy with the greatest pleasure what would be above the reach of any other creature of his small age." He was too delicate to be sent to school, but he was made to work hard at home till he was old enough to be sent to Cambridge. Although a very young man when he became a member of Parliament, his first speech in the House was a great success. "It is not a chip of the old block," said some one who heard him—"it is the old block himself;" meaning that this speech of young William Pitt was as good as any his father had made. When he first became Prime Minister he was only just twenty-four years old, and from that time until he died (twenty-four years afterwards) he was one of the most illustrious men in Europe. He and Wilberforce,* the last

* No. 20 on plan.

of the statesmen about whom I must tell you, were both very much interested in one thing—and this was the abolition of (or doing away with) slavery. The name of Wilberforce will never be forgotten, for he it was who first thought and said that slavery ought to be put an end to, all over the world, wherever Englishmen were the rulers. Wilberforce and William Pitt were once staying together in a country house not far from London, and sitting together one day under an old tree in the park, they began to talk about slavery, and to say how terrible a thing it was that the lives of hundreds and thousands of men and women and children were made full of misery by cruel masters who worked their slaves far harder than they worked their horses or their oxen. "I well remember," wrote Mr. Wilberforce in his Diary, "after this conversation with Mr. Pitt I resolved to give notice in the House of Commons of my intention to bring forward the abolition of the slave-trade."

And not long afterwards Wilberforce made a great speech in the House of Commons about slavery, and in the end a law was passed to do away with the slave-trade. Wherever the English flag was flying there should be no slavery, and a slave who could once set foot on any land held by Englishmen became a free man.

When Pitt died Wilberforce was one of those who carried a banner in the great funeral procession, when he was buried, as I have told you, in the same grave with his father, the first Pitt. Many years afterwards Wilberforce too "was buried there amongst his friends," and in another part of the Abbey there is a large statue of him, as an old and bent man, sitting in an armchair. When you go round the Abbey you must look for this monument, for it is said to be very like him during the last part of his life.

But we can spend no more time now in telling stories of statesmen, and must in the next chapter go on to the kings and queens.

CHAPTER V.

WE now come to the kings and queens who are buried in Westminster Abbey, and this will be the last chapter of my book.

You remember my telling you how Henry III. built a new shrine for Edward the Confessor. Three years after this Chapel of Edward the Confessor (as it is called) was finished, King Henry III.,* who had reigned for fifty-six years, died, and was buried in the Abbey which he had loved so long. His son Edward, who now became Edward I., was just starting home from the Holy Land with his wife, Queen Eleanor, who always went with him on all his journeys, when his father died, and he brought with him from the East the marble for the tomb.

I expect you will all remember having heard

* No. 21 on plan.

of this Queen Eleanor, the wife of Edward I. She was so brave and so fond of him that she would go with him when he went on his crusade to the Holy Land; and when people told her that it was dangerous, and that she might be killed, and tried to persuade her to stay at home, her only answer was, "The way to heaven is as near from Palestine as from England."

She was not killed, or even hurt; but there is a story told of how, while they were in the Holy Land, Edward was wounded by one of his enemies, who stabbed him in the arm with a poisoned dagger. This would certainly have killed him, if Eleanor had not at once sucked the poison out of the wound, and so saved his life.

Edward I.—Edward Longshanks, as he was called, for he was more than six feet high—and Queen Eleanor were crowned King and Queen of England in Westminster Abbey when they came back from the Holy Land. After the coronation a great banquet was given, to which Edward and his brother Edmund and all their nobles and attendants came—five hundred of them, riding on five hundred magnificent horses. When they dismounted, the horses were let loose in the crowd, and anybody who succeeded in catching one was allowed to keep it.

When, after having been Queen of England eighteen years, Eleanor * died at Hardby, in Nottinghamshire, her body was brought to Westminster, to be buried in the Abbey. From Nottinghamshire to London was a long journey in those days, and it had to be done by stages. Wherever the funeral procession stopped, Edward ordered a cross to be put up in memory of the queen. They were called the "Eleanor Crosses," and there were altogether twelve of them. The last was in London, at Charing Cross, which was the final halting-place before the procession reached the Abbey.

Edward I. was a great soldier, and gradually he "filled the Confessor's Chapel with trophies of war." One of these trophies you must

* No. 22 on plan.

specially notice when you go over the Abbey. At the west end of the Confessor's Chapel stand two chairs. One is a plain, very old-looking wooden chair, much scratched and battered, and underneath it is a rough-looking bit of stone. This old stone is called the "Stone of Scone," and on it all the Kings of Scotland had been crowned at Scone, which was the capital of Scotland up to the time when Edward I. became King of England. Edward I. and Alexander III., King of Scotland, were always at war; and when the English at last conquered the Scotch, Edward took away this ancient treasure, the "Stone of Scone," and brought it to Westminster Abbey, that our kings might be crowned upon it, as Kings of England and Scotland. The wooden chair was made by his orders, and the stone put underneath it, and there it has been ever since, for nearly six hundred years.

The other chair was made long afterwards for the coronation of William III. and Mary. Between the two are the sword and shield of

Edward III., which he is said to have used in all his many wars against France. The sword is seven feet long, and weighs eighteen pounds.

Edward I.,* "the greatest of the Plantagenets," was buried close by Queen Eleanor, but his tomb is quite plain. There is no figure on it, and no carving, as there is on the tombs of the other kings and queens. Dean Stanley explained, when he showed us the Abbey as children, that, for many years after Edward I. died, there was a kind of belief that, although the king was dead, yet, if another war broke out with Scotland, he would once again lead his army against the enemy, as he had so often done before. And so from time to time they would come and lift off the great marble slab which covered his tomb, and which was easily moved, and look in to see if the king was still there.

The first of our kings who was crowned on the "Stone of Scone" was Edward I.'s son, Edward II. He was crowned in the Abbey, but

* No. 23 on plan.

was not buried there. The next king who was buried there was Edward III.,* whose sword and shield we saw just now.

Richard II.,† the grandson of Edward III., is sometimes called the "Westminster King," because he was crowned and married and buried in the Abbey.

He was only eleven years old when he became King of England. For a week before his coronation he had lived in the Tower of London, which was the custom in those days for all kings and queens before they were crowned. The procession from the Tower to the Abbey was one of the most splendid that had ever been seen. But the service was very long, and the sermon was longer, and before it was over the king was carried out fainting. After this there was a great banquet, at which he had to appear again, and then at last the long day was over.

Five years later he was married in the Abbey to Queen Anne. After reigning for twenty-five

* No. 24 on plan.   † No. 25 on plan.

years, he was deposed by Henry of Lancaster, and murdered at Pontefract Castle in Yorkshire by his enemies—for he had made many during his life. He was buried in Hertfordshire. When Henry V. came to the throne, he ordered that Richard's body should be brought to Westminster, and then at last it was laid in the same tomb in which, many years before, his wife, Queen Anne, had been buried. Henry V.* when he was a boy was so wild that he was called "Madcap Harry." But he was particularly fond of the Abbey, and although most of his reign was spent in fighting with France, he did a great deal to improve and decorate his great church, and when the English won the battle of Agincourt (of which you may have heard or read), his first thought was to order a Thanksgiving Service to be held at Westminster. He had always said he wished to be buried in the Abbey; so, when he died in France his body was brought to England. "The

* No. 26 on plan.

long procession from Paris to Calais, and from Dover to London, was headed by the King of Scots, James I. . . . As it approached London it was met by all the clergy. The services were held first at St. Paul's, and then at the Abbey. No English king's funeral had ever been so grand. His three chargers were led up to the altar, behind the effigy (a wax model of the king carried outside his coffin), which lay on a splendid car, accompanied by torches and white-robed priests innumerable, . . and at the extreme eastern end of the Confessor's Chapel was deposited the body of the most splendid king that England had to that time produced."

Above his tomb, on a bar which stretches across the steps leading out of the chapel, are hung his helmet and saddle. The helmet is probably the very one which he wore at the battle of Agincourt, and which twice saved his life on that day; it is much dinted, and shows the marks of many sword-cuts.

Henry VI. was crowned king when he was

only nine years old, and on the day of his coronation it is said that he "sat on the platform in the Abbey beholding all the people about sadly and wisely." But as he was so young the service was shortened and he had much less to endure than the last boy-king, Richard II.

There is a story told of how, toward the end of his reign, King Henry VI. used to come and wander about in the Abbey between seven and eight o'clock in the evening, when it was growing dusk. He generally came quite alone, and only the abbot who carried a torch went with him round the dark and silent church. One night he went into the Confessor's Chapel, where he spent more than an hour, wondering if room could be, by-and-by, made for his own tomb. "It was suggested to him that the tomb of Henry V. should be pushed a little on one side, and his own placed beside it; but he replied, 'Nay, let him alone; he lieth like a noble prince; I would not trouble him.' But close beside the shrine of the Confessor there seemed to be room for another tomb. 'Lend me your staff,' he said to Lord Cromwell, who was with him that evening; 'is it not fitting I should have a place here, where my father and my ancestors lie, near St. Edward?' And then, pointing with a white staff to the place indicated, he said, 'Here, methinks, is a convenient place;' adding, 'Forsooth, forsooth, here will we lie; here is a good place for us.'" Three days afterwards the tomb was ordered to be made; but it was never even begun, for Henry was deposed by Edward IV. and died in the Tower, and from there his body was taken and buried in the Abbey of Chertsey.

Close by all these great kings and queens are several tombs of children. Among them is a monument to a little deaf and dumb girl of five years old, the Princess Catherine, daughter of Henry III. "Close to her, as if to keep her company, are buried her two little brothers, and four little nephews."

So far I have told you principally of kings

who are buried in Westminster Abbey, but now we come to the tombs of some of the Queens of England.

You remember that Henry VII. had built a great and magnificent chapel which was called after him. The first queen buried there was his wife, Queen Elizabeth, who was the mother of Henry VIII.

She had had a life full of adventures. She was the daughter of Edward IV., and sister of the two poor little princes who were murdered in the Tower by their uncle Richard.

Princess Elizabeth was born in Westminster, and christened in the Abbey, but she lived afterwards in the country at the palace of Sheen. When she was four years old, her father, Edward IV., was defeated in battle, and King Henry VI. was made King of England in his stead. The queen, the Princess Elizabeth, and her two baby sisters had to leave Sheen and come back to Westminster, where they were hidden in a place of safety while all these wars (the Wars of the Roses, as they were called) were going on. After two years, however, her father was victorious. Henry was deposed, and Edward IV. was once more King of England. To celebrate the victory, a great ball was given at Windsor Castle, and the little six-year-old princess, who was a special pet of her father's, came down and danced first with him, and then with some of the great nobles. When she was nine years old, her father and Louis XI., the King of France, decided that, as soon as she was grown up, she should marry the Dauphin, his eldest son, who, if he lived, would in time become the King of France. Then began a busy time for the little princess who might one day be Queen of France. Besides all her English lessons, she had to learn to speak and write French and Spanish, and she was always called "Madame la Dauphine," even while she was a little girl in the schoolroom. At last she was old enough to be married, but when the time for the wedding came, the King of France said he had found another wife for his son. Edward IV., who had set his heart on seeing his favourite daughter the Queen of France, was so disappointed and angry that he became very ill, and died. Then it was that Elizabeth's little brother Edward became Edward V., and the day was fixed for his coronation in the Abbey. A great banquet was arranged, and all the guests were invited; but before the day came, the little king and his younger brother, the Duke of York, were both killed by the order of their uncle, Richard, Duke of Gloucester, who then made himself King Richard III. of England. Now began a sad time for Princess Elizabeth, who was first taken away from her mother and sisters, and afterwards kept a prisoner in a lonely old castle in Yorkshire.

Meanwhile, during the time she was shut up here, many things had been going on about which she probably knew nothing.

Richard III. was hated by every one, and two years after he had become king, Henry, Earl of

Richmond, one of the greatest nobles in England, decided to try and depose him, and set free Princess Elizabeth. So he got together an army and marched to Leicester, where the king was then living. On the evening of a summer day the two armies camped at a place called Bosworth Field, and there the next day a great battle, the Battle of Bosworth, was fought, and Richard III. was killed. It is said that the crown of England had, at the beginning of the battle, been hidden in a hawthorn bush, and when afterwards it was found by a soldier, the Earl of Richmond was at once crowned King Henry VII., and all the soldiers who had been lying down, resting after the long fight, stood up round him and sang the *Te Deum*.

When Princess Elizabeth, in her far-away lonely castle, heard cries of joy from the people who came crowding to the doors of her prison she guessed that something had happened and that a better time might be coming for her. And soon came a messenger from the king, who had been sent straight from the field of battle, with orders to set the princess free and bring her to London.

The end of this story is really almost like the end of a fairy tale, for her many troubles were now over, and the next year she married Henry VII., and so became Queen of England. And when after many years she died, she was buried —as I told you at the beginning of this story— in the Chapel of Henry VII. in Westminster Abbey. Some years later the king was buried beside her; and inside the bronze railings surrounding the tomb (which stands behind the altar) you will see the figures of Henry VII.* and his wife, Queen Elizabeth, lying side by side.

Three other queens who are buried here are known to all of you. Two of them were sisters, Queen Mary † and Queen Elizabeth, ‡ the daughters of Henry VIII.; and the third was their cousin, another Mary—Mary Queen of Scots,§ who was beheaded by the order of Queen

---

* No. 27 on plan.   † No. 28 on plan.
‡ Also No. 28 on plan.   § No. 29 on plan.

Elizabeth, because she was afraid that Mary wanted to make herself Queen of England in her stead. Queen Mary and Queen Elizabeth, though they were sisters, had all their lives been enemies. They differed about everything, but especially about their religion, for Mary had been brought up a Roman Catholic, and Elizabeth and their little brother Edward (who afterwards became Edward VI.) were Protestants. Elizabeth and Edward were very fond of one another, and it is said that Elizabeth used to spend a great deal of her time when she was quite a little girl in doing needlework for her brother. On his second birthday she gave him for a birthday present a little shirt which she had made for him all herself, though she was then only six years old.

Both these queens, when little girls, were made to do a great many lessons, and were taught Latin and Greek with their brother, as well as French and Italian and Spanish. Queen Mary was always very fond of music, and there is a story told of how, when she was only three years old, some friends of her father's (King Henry VIII.) came down to see her at Richmond, where she was then living. The little princess—for this was a long time before she became queen—was not in the least shy: she welcomed her visitors, and after talking to them "and entertaining them with most goodly countenance"—for so one of the gentlemen who was there wrote about her afterwards—she played to them on the virginal (a kind of piano), after which strawberries and biscuits and wine were brought in, and the baby princess had nothing more to do but enjoy herself. These three children, Mary, Elizabeth, and Edward, became in turn Queens and King of England.

When Henry VIII. died, Edward, the youngest of the three, became King Edward VI. But he had all his life been very delicate, and when he had been king just six years, and was sixteen years old, he died, and then Mary, his eldest sister, became queen. The reign of Queen Mary—Bloody Mary she is sometimes called—

was a terrible time in England, for, as I told you, she was a Roman Catholic, and so determined was she that all English men and women should be Roman Catholics too, that she ordered those who were Protestants to change their religion and become Catholics; and if they refused, they were burnt alive. Hundreds of people were killed in this cruel way; and Queen Mary became at last so much hated, that when she died, and the Princess Elizabeth became queen, there was rejoicing almost all over England. For in spite of all the queen had done to make England a Roman Catholic country, by far the greater part of the people had remained Protestants, and now once again had a Protestant queen to reign over them.

Almost the last time a Catholic Mass (or service) was held in Westminster Abbey was at the funeral of Queen Mary.* The procession, led by the monks, who knew that this was most

* The last Catholic funeral service was held in the Abbey a few days later, when by the order of Elizabeth a requiem mass was said for the Emperor Charles V.

likely the last service in which they would ever take part, came from St. James's Palace, where she died, down to Westminster, and at the great West Door of the Abbey were waiting four bishops and the Abbot of Westminster in all the magnificent robes which Catholic priests wear.

The body of the queen was carried into Henry VII.'s chapel, and all night the Abbey was dimly lighted by the hundred wax torches which were held and kept alight by the soldiers of the Queen's Guard. The next day she was buried, and the Catholic Bishop of Winchester preached before Elizabeth, who, although she hated the religion, did not refuse to come to the funeral of her sister, as Queen Mary had done years before on the death of their brother Edward, when, rather than come to a Protestant service in the Abbey, she ordered a separate funeral mass to be said before her in the Tower.

A little more than a month after this, Queen Elizabeth was crowned in the Abbey, and for the next forty-five years "good Queen Bess," as she is often called, reigned over England, and did much that was wise and good. One thing she did, however, that was neither wise nor good, and that one thing I spoke about when I told you that two Queen Marys were buried here, one of whom was Mary Queen of Scots, the cousin of Elizabeth. The story of Mary Queen of Scots is a long and very sad one. You will some day read about her, if you have not already done so, and when you hear how she was imprisoned in Fotheringay Castle, and at last beheaded, you will perhaps feel that in some ways Elizabeth could be as cruel as her sister Mary.

These three queens are all buried in Henry VII.'s Chapel—Elizabeth and Mary together in a white marble tomb, on the outside of which lies the statue of Queen Elizabeth, and on which these words in Latin were written by James I.: "Consorts both in throne and grave, here rest we two sisters, Elizabeth and Mary, in hope of our resurrection." And not far from them lies Mary Queen of Scots. After she had been beheaded at Fotheringay Castle her body was buried in

Peterborough Cathedral, and from there it was brought to Westminster by her son, James VI. of Scotland, who was also James I. of England, "that the like honour," so he wrote, "might be done to his dearest mother," as had been done to Queen Elizabeth and the other Queen Mary.

We are now coming to the end of these stories, and I must only mention in a very few words some of the other graves in this chapel of Henry VII.

Oliver Cromwell * who, after Charles I. had been beheaded, made himself Protector of England, was buried here among the kings and queens. It is said that his funeral was more magnificent than any king's had ever been, and that an immense sum of money was spent upon it. Close by him was buried Elizabeth Claypole, his favourite daughter, and many of his soldiers and followers.

Three years afterwards his body was dug up and taken to Tyburn. There his head was cut off, on the 30th of January, the anniversary of the day Charles I. had been beheaded, after

* No. 30 on plan.

which his body was buried under the gallows, instead of in Westminster Abbey.

"Here are also buried," says Dean Stanley, "some of our young princes and princesses. There was that wonderfully gifted boy, Edward VI."* (of whom we have already spoken), "who was only sixteen when he died, and who before that time had by his diligence and his honesty made himself beloved and trusted by all about him. There is the good Prince Henry, eldest son of James I., who when his foolish attendants provoked him to swear because a butcher's dog had killed a stag that he was hunting, said, 'Away with you! All the pleasure in the world is not worth a profane oath.' Then there was, again, that other Henry, Duke of Gloucester, who sat on the knees of his father, Charles I., on the day before his execution, and who when his father said to him, 'They will try to make you king instead of your elder brother,' fired up like a little man, and said, 'I will be torn in pieces first!' Then there are two small tombs

* No. 31 on plan.

of the two infant daughters of James I. (one of which is made in the shape of a cradle). And to these tombs of these two little girls were brought, in after-days, by King Charles II., the bones of the two young murdered princes (Edward V. and Richard, Duke of York), which in his time were discovered at the foot of the staircase in the Tower. Well might all these princes be mourned and have a place in this Abbey, because many of them, though they died early, showed of what stuff they were made, and that they would have been fit to be kings and to be with kings."

As I copied down these words of Dean Stanley's, I was once more reminded of him, and once more I seemed to hear him telling the children gathered round him in the Abbey some of these stories which I have just been telling you. And as the last words in this book about the Abbey are his words, so the last grave which I want to tell you of is his, and when you some day go to the Abbey you must not forget to see (also in Henry VII.'s Chapel) the place where, together in one tomb, are buried Arthur Stanley,* Dean of Westminster, and his wife, Lady Augusta.

Dean Stanley knew more about Westminster Abbey than almost any other man; and not only did he *know* more, but by writing books and by telling stories to his friends as he showed them over the great church, he helped many other people, who but for him perhaps would not have thought much about the Abbey at all to know something of the Church of St. Peter on Thorney Isle.

And it is because I hoped that what interested us as children many years ago might interest others now, that I have tried to remember, and collect, and write down these tales from Westminster Abbey in something the same way as they were told to us by the Dean.

* No. 32 on plan.

THE END.

RETURN TO the circulation desk of any
University of California Library
or to the
NORTHERN REGIONAL LIBRARY FACILITY
Bldg. 400, Richmond Field Station
University of California
Richmond, CA 94804-4698

ALL BOOKS MAY BE RECALLED AFTER 7 DAYS
- 2-month loans may be renewed by calling (510) 642-6753
- 1-year loans may be recharged by bringing books to NRLF
- Renewals and recharges may be made 4 days prior to due date.

DUE AS STAMPED BELOW

SENT ON ILL

JAN 10 2000

U. C. BERKELEY

12,000 (11/95)

M309230

ImTheStory.com

Personalized Classic Books in many genre's

Unique gift for kids, partners, friends, colleagues

Customize:
- Character Names
- Upload your own front/back cover images (optional)
- Inscribe a personal message/dedication on the inside page (optional)

Customize many titles Including
- Alice in Wonderland
- Romeo and Juliet
- The Wizard of Oz
- A Christmas Carol
- Dracula
- Dr. Jekyll & Mr. Hyde
- And more...

SD - #0030 - 210722 - C0 - 229/152/6 - PB - 9781314473896 - Gloss Lamination